When Wives Fight Families Win

MELTORIA WOODSIDE

ISBN 978-1-64028-052-6 (Paperback)
ISBN 978-1-64028-053-3 (Digital)

Christian Faith Publishing, Inc.
296 Chestnut Street
Meadville, PA 16335
www.christianfaithpublishing.com

Printed in the United States of America

Contents

Introduction

The institution of marriage is bound to come under an attack of some sort from the enemy. However, the result does not have to be divorce. When infidelity attacked my marriage, it was devastating; I could not see a clear path to happiness, peace, or comfort. No one was there to tell me, to hang in, or to encourage me to push through. In fact, I did not have an example I could look to for hope. The only thing I had to push me was my love for my husband and family; with that motivation, I called onto Holy Spirit, who is my helper. He guided me and protected me through the storm and led me to a victorious marriage.

As a married woman, you should learn to be proactive in the war against marriages and to cover your husband and your marriage in prayer before the enemy strikes. This book will heighten your awareness of the enemy's plans and tactics that are set out against the marriage institution.

I believe this book will not only benefit people who are facing marital issues but also those who are divorced and those who intend to remarry one day. The Bible declares that we must be aware of the devices of the enemy.

If you are reading this book and you intend to marry, you will identify issues even before marriage. That way, you can have a better judgment if you want to make a person your lifelong partner or soulmate. I try my best to tell every wife fight, but many find it hard to fight or press through a storm where there is no strong foundation. When I fought, I understood that I was not only fighting for my husband, but I was also fighting for, my friend, the rest of me.

The strategies that are outlined in his book are strategies I used under the direction of the Holy Spirit, who led me to victory. Many people who divorce are divorced because they thought it was the solution, the only option, or it was the best thing to do. However, after reading this book, you will learn that when you remarry and trouble hits again, that there is another way. You can fight and be victorious because divorce is not a solution; it is a plan of the enemy.

In the Beginning...

Just a little background, I am from the beautiful Bahamas Islands but live in sunny California. My husband and I were dating from high school. We knew each other before we attended the same high school, but just as another neighbor on the island. In the late eighties, we both went to the same primary school, but I would be lying if I said we even looked in each other's direction. In fact, my second year of high school, I had absolutely no interest in him, but he was in hot pursuit of me. He was a very persistent young man, I might add. I was young and not attracted to him. I always had in my head I would *never* like someone who is taller than me, and he was a tall fella.

When Yocasta moved to my neighborhood during our high school years, I was the only one he knew at the time. We became good friends and hung out a lot, both in school and out of school. During this period, we became close in our friendship; I did not like him other than as a friend, but he became attracted to me at some point. Although not attracted to him physically, I found attraction in his pursuit of me. It was the summer of 1995 when I gave in to his pursuit and the dating began. When we returned to school after the summer, the entire school was shocked we were dating. Some were angry and accuse me of once saying we were cousins: "So how can they be going?" (dating).

As young as we were, I truly had no interest in a husband, and I never said to myself I would marry him! However, weeks passed, months passed years passed, and we were still together. After dating for five years, we had a son together, then a few months after that, later in the year 2000, we got married. The Bible declares in Proverbs 18:22 (Aramaic Bible) in plain English, "He that finds a wife finds a good thing and receives the will of the Lord Jehovah, and he that puts away a good wife puts away a good thing from his house". My wedding day was amazing! I felt the happiness in the air and everyone felt it was about time we tied the knot. Our wedding left a good taste on the community as it was beautiful!

Infidelity Uncovered

I have heard many horror stories about marriage, but I felt special as I was experiencing a good life, a happy marriage. My marriage was considered what some people called a dream marriage. My beloved husband praised me wherever he went. I was well treated and loved. I felt like a queen! I can remember mentioning to my sister, "The Lord knows why He gave me a good husband, because I can't take much." Well, six years into our marriage, we were expecting baby boy number 2. This baby, I wanted; I was just ready for more kids. I was super excited and was counting down the time before I met the new addition to our happy family.

While at work one day, going about my usual routine, I felt a sharp pain in my abdomen and had to be airlifted to the hospital. We lived on a small island; the local clinic was not taking any risk with my pains as I was about eight months pregnant and the clinic was not equipped to deliver a baby. I was forced into maternity leave earlier than expected. Well, here is where it gets interesting. I was at the doctor's clinic attending my regular maternity visit, the visit after they took culture samples to ensure that the baby was fine despite the sharp pains I experienced. Now when I got there, the nurse or the doctor's assistant pulled me aside with my file to give me my test results. She opened the file and pointed to one of my test results that said "POSITIVE." Okay, now it did not register immediately, but I kept looking back and forth as the assistant rubbed my back, consoling me. When it sank in, I wept; I HAD AN STD (curable, thank God)! Now I do not have a college education, but I would like to believe I was a smart woman. I asked what I thought was the stupidest question on earth, "Is there another way to get an STD?".

Now the assistant was just as bad as me because she answered no. The doctor himself tried to console me, telling me, ".Mrs Woodside, do not be upset. Sometimes the disease can be from a previous relationship". That just made matters worse—a previous relationship? We have been together since high school!

Hours had not even passed before the devil started to torment me; thoughts in my mind was going a mile a minute. He whispered in my ear, "LEAVE HIM!" At that moment, felt like the gates of hell had opened against me; my head became flooded with crazy thoughts I couldn't even put into perspective. I was so naive. I couldn't even think of whom my husband may have been cheating with. Almost nine months pregnant, there was no way I should have to be dealing with this. I was in the doctor's office when I called my husband to tell him this interesting discovery. I was acting calm on the phone when I asked him, but Lord knows my heart was crying out loud. Who? "Who?" was the question of the hour. When my husband revealed who it was, my stomach broke down. This girl he told me was dating another friend of his, someone that went on family trips with us! Infidelity in my house was in plain sight.

One day, as we were talking and He was trying to console me, I got this strange feeling, a feeling that spoke and said, "She is pregnant." Now, this could just be the hormones talking, so I did give it that much thought. As I was patiently waiting time for my baby boy to arrive, I tried to avoid talking about my husband's infidelity to my in-laws. So one day, they were talking in what they thought were codes; however, I knew what they were talking about. They were saying they heard a certain girl was pregnant, and who she was pregnant for was the surprise. I went about my routine acting like I was in the dark, but I was crying inside. I felt as if the world was against me; shame and embarrassment would not allow me to reveal to them (I KNOW). I was so naïve; this young lady ate from my pot. She was having my food and my husband for dinner. The thought of it all pierced my heart like a dagger. Lord, what have I done?

Decision to Fight

I left the doctor's office with my eyes bloodshot from crying. My sister-in-law was with me and asked, "Is everything okay?"

I am usually a private person, so I was not about to tell my sister-in-law that I found out her brother was cheating on me. "Yes" I answered; that was a tough visit, a very tough visit! As the moments passed, I was in a daze. My life was playing in my head; I was thinking of all the great moments we had. All the happy times flooded my mind in the middle of it all. Then I asked the Lord, "Lord, what do I do?" I thought to myself, *Do I give up all the happy times and throw it down the drain for this one sad moment, or do I push through?* I made up in my mind that I would just push through. However, I had no idea what that meant. I had no clue what lay ahead for me and my family. Even though I said I would push through, it was very hard even in that moment as I was almost ready to deliver my baby.

With all the hormone imbalance, along with my broken heart, my head was not in a good space. My self-esteem went down the toilet. I began to feel worthless. Yes, I had a moment of happy thoughts but then, the enemy came into my head, whispering that all this time, I was living a lie. I was feeling he was correct; I had no idea how this happened to me. I didn't even see or feel it coming. How could I have been so happy? I was being cheated on with no warning; it was all in plain sight, but I did not see. I thought, *You know what, I will live without him. I will take care of my kids without him.* However, that was not a reality as my love for my husband ran deep.

I was keeping all the pain in, not sharing it with anyone because I was so ashamed, but I needed to talk to someone. I picked up the phone and called my pastor. I told him what I found out and one of the first questions he asked was, "Well, Sister Meltoria, what are you going to do?" He continued, "You have to make a decision: will you end your marriage over this, or will you stay and fight?"

I said, "Pastor, I am not going to leave. I will fight!"

With all confidence, I made up in my mind that I was not going to lose my good husband over this. I thought to myself, *I did not want to be a divorcee this young. I do not want to find another husband.* My mind was going a mile a minute with good and bad thoughts. I thought about my kids and their future. I did not physically know another man, so how do I go and find someone else? Deciding to fight for my marriage was a big step, but what was ahead I could not see coming.

As the days passed, it was time for me to deliver my second son. This should have been a happy moment for me, and it was, but it came in the middle of so much sorrow. My heart was not filled with joy as one would be in welcoming a new baby. I spent three nights in the hospital, and every night, my husband was there. When I was admitted, it was as if both my husband and I we're admitted to the hospital because he stayed the entire time. I am telling you, he never left the hospital, not even to shower! From the moment I delivered our son, he was with me, supportive as ever. When one would be thinking how blessed I was, I was thinking of my pain and revenge. I was thinking that I should have denied him this opportunity; I should call security and make him leave. Lord knows that was not what I wanted, but I sure was thinking on it. I may have been very mad, upset, and hurt, but we all know I was still very much in love.

My son was born in Vero Beach, Florida. After he was delivered, and some time had passed, it was time for us to move back to my hometown, which is Abaco, Bahamas. When we were in Vero Beach, things were not that bad; of course I was feeling a lot of hurt, pain, and anger. However, when I went back home after having the baby, reality set in. Yes, I decided to fight; however, I had no idea what exactly that meant. As I was at home recovering from having my new baby, things began to get very difficult. Anger was really setting in, torment was setting in, unrest was setting in. I began to feel disconnected with my new baby as I was feeling some type of resentment and regret on having him. I kind of blame the fact that I never noticed my husband's infidelity on my pregnancy. I was still angry, but I could not freak out on anyone because I was a new mom. Every time my husband left the house, I was worrying, "Is he with her?" I had a friend of mine playing secret agent, putting her well-being in danger. Many times I wanted to go out to investigate, but I couldn't because I had a new baby.

Initially, when I found out my husband was unfaithful, he was very remorseful and the fact that he was trying to comfort me and let me know that the girl meant nothing to him, and it was a one-time thing. However, as I continued to be super detective wife, I began to uncover some things that I had not known. I found evidence that he was communicating with this young lady long before his infidelity was discovered. I confronted him with lots of evidence and findings. All the evidence proved that what he was saying about the one-time thing was a lie. I even took it upon myself to have a one-on-one conversation with her by telephone, of course. The things she told me were so heartbreaking it crushed me and didn't make me feel any better as I look back. She told me I was living in a bubble; my husband only loved for me when he was in our house, but when he steps out of that zone, he loved her! Can you imagine hearing this load of crap? This was a good moment for me to trip out. So much time had passed from the moment I found out till that moment were on the phone. I spent so much time crying I was weak; I didn't even have strength to trip out on no one. I did tell him what she was saying, and if my memory serves me correctly, the only thing hubby said was, "She wish."

It was really hard for me to believe he did not love her; as much pain as he saw me in, he still continued to see her! I had the thought in my head that she was the one girl that caused him to step out on me; she must have had some power over him.

As time passed, my husband began to act very different to me; he was not as loving and comforting as he once was. I concluded that it was the pressure of dealing with my misery. Well, my maternity leave was over, and it was time to return to work. The days of being home drowning in my sorrow had come to an end. I am a private person, so I was not about to return to work looking pitiful. The island where I lived was small, so everyone knew what I was dealing with. After all, this young girl was parading around showing off the fact that she was pregnant for my husband. When I returned to work, I felt welcomed; I made it a point to consume myself with my job that I would forget what was going on at home. However, the sad part was, I only worked from eight to five so that moment of comfort was always temporary.

I was always a simple gal, a little ChapStick on the lips, hair fixed, and I was ready to go. Things had changed, though, as this whole infidelity thing took a toll on my self-esteem. I felt worthless; my confidence had died and went to heaven. I tried to take a new approach to try look beautiful, by investing in lots of makeup. I went from wearing a natural look, to a full-blown doll face. I wore the whole nine yards—foundation, press powder, blush, eyeshadow, eye and lip liner, and mascara—every day! The response I was getting from my co-workers was, "Wow, you look beautiful." I should feel better by that, but truth of the matter was, it was a mask to hide my true feelings; I was a wreck! One of my co-workers came to me and asked, "Mel, with all the hell you going through, how do you manage to look like nothing is happening?"

My only response was a smile, but the real answer was, "What you see was fake!" I looked good at work, but when I went home, I was dredged in my sorrow. Every time someone asked me how I was doing, I would answer "great" with a big smile. This was my reality for quite some time; I was living a double life, operating from two personalities.

One day, my sister-in-law came to me and said, "Toya, I have something to tell you. I know you won't believe it, but I have to tell you anyway. I cannot stand to see you go through what you are going through."

My heart should have dropped, but I already felt that I have already heard the worst. Another young lady told her my husband was trying to get with her, and she was feeling so sorry for me; she wanted to tell someone, so she went to my sister-in-law. My hands began to shake uncontrollably; my joints began to ache. I thought to myself, *This cannot be real!* Yes, my sister-in-law was correct; I would not believe it. Not that I don't think my husband is capable, but after you know the pain I am currently going through with what you call a past situation, you are going to make something new. Well, this lady was well prepared to expose my husband; she went to the extent of giving me access to her voicemail to hear my husband trying to arrange time to meet up with her. The voicemail was too explicit for me to go into, but to make matters worst, my baby who was about three months at the time was in the background. See, while I went to work, hubby was home with the baby as he was unemployed at the time. I dropped to the floor and wept! Lord, have mercy on my soul. Why is this happening to me? I did not want to confront my husband in the heat of the moment, so I waited until I calmed all the way down.

So when I got home, we had houseguests; his parents were over. This was not a good time to confront hubby, but I could not contain it any longer. I met him in our bedroom and asked him nicely, "Honey, do you know this young lady because she said you were trying to talk to her?"

Off course he denied it and blamed it on, "Everyone will try say he wanted to talk to them after all this."

Well, I pushed it, "Are you sure!" While I was asking that, I proceeded to pull up the voicemail for him to hear. His voice barely made it on the phone; he launched and slapped me across the face. I fell straight to the floor. Now as I said earlier, the in-laws were over, and being the private person that I am, I swallowed the noise and cried out loud silently. My husband never laid a hand on me; neither did he ever attempt to do so in all our eleven years together. Just as fast as lightning could strike, I was looking at a stranger.

My nightmare just started all over again. I said I will forgive my husband for one mistake, but what was I really facing? My beloved husband whom I shared my soul with was no longer only interested in me. He was lusting after God knows who. What will I be fighting for? Apart from my marriage falling apart, and my husband having multiple affairs, he was also careless in our finances. My husband was in the banking industry, so he controlled all our finances. We always believed that it was his responsibility to take care of the home. For years, I never paid a bill; in fact, I had no clue what bills we had. All I knew was we had utilities (off course), were homeowners (which meant a mortgage), and we owned a nice car (car payment). However, all this was coming to an end; we were about to lose our home to the bank and we were delayed in our payments. When I heard this, I was lost for words; see, we had tenants who paid their rent every month. I was working a good job and was making enough to keep our house together; we only needed a few bucks from my pay to put with the tenant's rent to keep the mortgage current. However, somehow, something was not going right. I remember one day hubby pulled me in the room and said he has something to tell me. Honestly, I was numb at this point in my life; nothing would surprise me. He told me that he had gambled all the tenant's rent. The news did not move me one bit. I was immune to bad news; in fact, I had no more tears to spare.

Night after night, after I put the kids to bed and hubby was out, I spent crying. I was feeling so bad I just wanted to die; now I know suicide was not an option, but the thought of dying in a bad accident was something I welcomed. One night, I kneeled in my bed and began to cry out to my Lord, "Jesus, help me." At this time, I was a youth leader and dance minister at my local church; you would think I knew how to pray. With all the pain I was going through, the only words I could have utter in time of prayer was "Jesus, help me," "Lord, I need you!" Over and over, I cried these words unto the Lord (Jeremiah 33:3): "Call unto me, and I will answer thee, and shew thee great and mighty things which thou knowest not."

Well, with all the crazy that was going on in our lives, we were about to lose our home, but before that happened, we got someone to purchase it. We sold our home and moved in with the in-laws, who had a large-enough home that could accommodate us. I was not so happy about it at first because I know our marriage was on the crazy lane, but I embraced it anyway. Life did not get any better than it was, I might add. I did cry less though, but it was because I was all cried out. I just did not have anything in me to let out. Did I think it was all out and over? I sure did. Perhaps we were bringing this sinking ship into the harbor.

Not long living with the in-laws, my sister-in-law had more news; well, she was not so certain about this information, but she told me anyway. She heard that her brother was involved with yet another! My heart took another blow as I felt like an even bigger fool. This young lady that my sister-in-law mentioned to me about, I saw my husband with her a few times, but it looked innocent and I was in my overconfident space. I attempted to investigate the matter and ask the young lady about it, but she did not give me the time of day to talk to her. She accused me of trying to destroy her family as mine is destroyed. With no luck there, I decided to confront my husband about this. Now I never go before him without hard evidence, but I had none. I asked him about this other girl, girl no. 3, not 3 as in that is the order she fell in his extramarital relationships, but no. 3 as in the third person I found out about. Should I have confronted him without evidence; after all, I honestly did not think he would tell the truth. Well, as always, I waited until I was calm. I asked him, "Honey, I heard you were going with this girl, is it true?"

"Who told you that?" he asked.

Now I really did not want to get my sis-in-law in trouble so I told him, "Do not worry who told me. Just answer my question."

Well, he was more concerned about who told me than whether it was untrue. I tried to hold my ground; I was not trying to tell him whom I got the information from. Well, the next thing I know, I got struck so hard in my stomach I could not breathe. I fell to the floor trying to catch my breath, but here it goes again, another hit straight in my mouth and busted my lip. I was no match; I told him his sister. Well, there was still no answer to the question, but after the blows, I did not think to press.

Now, here is what made things difficult for me— being the private person that I was and living with peo-ple. I have a busted lip; of course people would ask what happened, and I was not about to say "My hus-band hit me," so I covered it up with some lie. I was crying inside, my chest was hurting, my breaths were short, just trying to make it another day, hoping that when I wake up this nightmare would be over. It was easy to get pass his family, but my sister was not buying no dumb story; in fact, I did not even try to cover it up with her. I told her the truth. Some time before all this happened, my sister said she dreamed I was being abused. Well, off course it was not true at the time. I always thought my family was under the impression that I was being abused, but really, at that time, I was living the good life, or so I thought. Well, my beloved sister was not even giving me a chance to put up with that crap. She came and picked me up from work and marched me straight into the courthouse.

She said, "Come, let us go get a restraining order. I will not have him hitting up on you, no way!" Well, I did get all the paperwork and kept it at my office, but really, I did not want to leave on the account that my sister pushed me so I held on to the papers in case I needed it. In fact, just after the lip-busting incident, hubby consoled me and apologized for it. With my soft heart, I accepted his apology in a heartbeat; I truly thought that it will never happen again.

Love Child

The community where I lived was small, so I often ran into my beloved's lover. She proudly paraded her pumpkin belly. She did not have to do much explaining on who the expected baby's father was as everyone knew. She was very proud that she was carrying my beloved's love child. Every day after finding out about my beloved's unfaithfulness was painful, but every time I saw his lover was even worse. I knew the day would come when love child came to grace the land, so I tried mentally preparing myself for that day. Early on, I have decided that I would not allow this to ruin my marriage, so accepting love child was inevitable.

What a time of my life I never saw this coming. One day, the sun was shining so bright upon my life, and in a blink of an eye, dark clouds were hanging over me. Early one morning, hubby was sitting up, and I was still asleep. As I rolled over and looked at him, he was in a daze. I asked him, "What happened, honey?"

"She had the baby," he answered. My heart collapsed, but I just laid in my bed; just another day has been added to the saddest days of my life. Usually, you hear about one day being the saddest day, but I had many saddest days.

About two weeks had gone past, and I have not heard anything about this baby until one night, hubby was at the computer listening to music. I was sitting in the bed just lying in a daze. I looked up and saw hubby basically fuming at the mouth! With a complete shock in my eyes, I asked him what happened. He took a few minutes before he replied, but when he did, nothing good came out his mouth. He began to call me every name in the book other than a child of God. My eyes tore wide open! I did not utter a word, but I thought, "What!" Even at my worst, I have never done anything for him to call me these words or see me in this manner. He said that his son has been born two weeks ago, and he has not seen him yet. I was so shocked; yes, his son has been born two weeks ago, and he did not see him, but how is that my problem? As I was silent, the tears just rolled down my cheeks; my heart beat slowly. It was late, and the kids were with the in-laws; I laid my head on my pillow with hope that I would gain strength to face the next day.

Just a few days after the outburst, my beloved decided he was going to take the trip and go and meet his love child. During that time, my beloved was unemployed, so I was not sure where he was getting funds from to visit his love child. However, at our family's expense, he made a way. As I woke the next day, I put on my mask and headed to work. It was the end of the week and a pay day. I never rush to the bank as I was not accustomed to paying our bills. However, this particular day, I decided to see if our payroll had reached the bank as yet. Well, I got the shock of my life; not only did the pay reach the bank, but mine was already tapped into. There was almost nothing left. Well, I was not too alarmed, so I asked hubby what he did with the money; well, he had made plans to head out of town to see his son! My heart left me; I was stunned. You took just about all our funds to go see your son with this girl? What about our needs? What will we do until I get paid again? He did not care about us; it is obvious!

I have two kids here to take care of, and you are going to take food out of their mouth. *I must stop him*, I thought to myself. However, I was not told when he was going to take this trip. Early the next morning, he got up, packing things in a bag. I asked him, "Are you really going?" He said nothing to me and just proceeded with his business. I tried to stop him; I tried to hang onto him as he went in the car. However, he dragged me; this was a losing battle for me, so I let him loose. His love child was not on the island as yet and was already creating an issue. This was not sitting well with me and was causing me to have ill feelings toward him. All the time I spent mentally preparing for his arrival had gone out the window. At this time now, I said to myself I want no part of love child's life.

As I proceed into the house, I felt something cold running down my legs. My body was under so much stress, I just began to bleed out. I went in my bed and just rested. I was losing hope in this thing called marriage I am going to leave this man. As I was alone in my room, I felt a need to just pray. I got on my knees and began to cry out. "In the name of Jesus, I bind divorce and separation (Matthew 18:18). I decree and declare that this marriage will not fail. Lord, bind us together with unity, with cords that cannot be broken."

It was the weekend, so I spent most of it by my sister. I did not share with her what I had just gone through, just that Hubby went to see his son and will be back the following day. I was acting like nothing happened, but inside I was shattered like glass. I went to church that Sunday just like every other Sunday; a few people asked me how I was doing, and of course, my favorite answer was "I am okay." No matter how I was doing, I stuck with that. As we know by now, I may be a wreck, but I was not wearing wreckage on my face.

One day, as I was out with my beloved for lunch, I caught a glimpse of beloved's lover. Apparently, she had just finished up from taking love child to his doctor's visit. As I brought her to beloved's attention, he asked me if I wanted to see the baby. I am so tender-hearted; I said, "Sure." At the same time, I was calling myself crazy in my own head. As we drove around the corner to her house, so much mixed feelings was going on in my head. However, I challenged myself to keep it together; it was a must for me.

As we pulled up to the house, she came outside. Beloved said to her that we were there to see the baby. She did not look so happy with the idea as she gave us the side eye. Little did she know, I was not happy either. My beloved asked if I wish to hold the baby, but

I refused. It was too early for me; I did not trust myself! In fact, as my beloved held love child, I could see him dropping him in the rocky grounds. It was such an evil thought; I rolled my eyes at myself thinking I was not that lucky.

As months had passed, I really tried to do my best and to do what I thought may be pleasing to God and what may be the right thing to do for the child. Since my beloved was unable to financially provide for love child, I offered that we do it together. It was a bold step, given the fact that we were not in a good position financially, but I was willing to sacrifice to ensure that love child's needs were met. As I bought for my kids, I would get something for love child; it was in no way an easy thing to do. Buying pampers was a budget breaker and having to buy two sets was a killer. Now as God and hubby as my witness I was pushing through. I thought that hubby and I were moving forth and doing this thing together until rumor surfaced! It came to my attention that this young lady was spreading news that my husband was taking my hard-earned money and taking care of her son. Now as far as I knew, we were both taking care of him together, but apparently, something else was going on behind my back. I was confused why.

I did not want to cut my beloved off from accessing my hard-earned money, but it looked like it was necessary. Not that I did not want to provide for love child, but I did not like being taken advantage of. So the following week, I took the necessary steps to ensure that my wages were not going to the joint bank account of my beloved and me. When beloved found out what I done, he was furious. However, he then realized that was he was doing to me was unjust. Again, let me say, I am tender-hearted. After my beloved gave what I felt was a sincere apology, I had my wages reverted back to our joint account. No matter how understanding I tried to be, hurt and pain still found their way in my path. The existence of love child was driving me out of right-mind zone. I was looking to go loco any moment. Thinking about my beloved being a father to a child outside my home was a pill I have yet to swallow. I never spoke or expressed my feelings to anyone; in silence I wept.

Our community was small, and oftentimes, I would come past love child and his mom. It looked as if she was having a hard time providing for him by the clothes he wore. It really touched my soft spot. Although love child's mom was not my favorite person, I was not about to use love child as a pawn in battle. The love child was no longer an infant, so I felt that if he is living in our home, we can better ensure he is provided for. Our house was not living in the overflow; what we had been just enough for the house. However, if love child was there, he would not miss out on anything my kids had. I asked love child's mom if he could live with us; she was more than happy.

Just a few months later, I, too, lost my job. I was blindsided and devastated by this loss. It was what was keeping our family afloat. Well, now only my beloved was working, and his income was small. I was not about to be struggling with my two kids and his love child. That same day, I called his mom and told her we can no longer keep him. During one of our counseling sessions before love child was born, my pastor gave my beloved some real sound advice. He said, "Yes, this is your child, but your priority is to your home." At that time, that did not mean too much to me, but when we got in a place where we were barely making ends meet, it all made sense. Since my beloved was not in a position to support his family and love child, what was he to do?

Months later, love child and his mom moved off the island, and we were out of contact. We were unable to provide for love child financially, so the love child's mother was not interested in any other communication. It is my opinion that love child's mom was still young and immature and did not understand that there is something that exists that is far more valuable than money and that is time and relationship. During that time, my beloved and I thought that it was time for us to make a change. Things on the island were not looking positive for us, so we needed to explore other options for our family. We had the opportunity to move to the United States, and without questions, we took it. For me, I was a bit happy to leave because I needed a change of environment. I was also happy because I knew we were moving far away from love child.

Yes, even though love child was some years old, issues still existed. I was still unsettled about his existence. Sharing my kids' father with another child was not easy to embrace. Often I prayed and asked God to fix my heart so I can grow to love him like my own. I did not hate him, but I did not love him and I know that was a problem I needed to work on. Now my family and I were settled into our new home, and somehow, love child never left my mind as I thought. I was always thinking about him and his well-being. Or cautious about how him and his father's lack of relationship would affect him. There were times I wanted to reach out to love child's mom to inquire about him, but I did not need to encounter her crazy energy. As long as she did not reach out to us, I would not reach out to her. Yes, I thought about love child often, but I was okay with the lack of communication.

At some point, love child's mom woke up to the reality side of the bed and decided to reach out to my beloved. She messaged him through Facebook Messenger to basically tell him, "Hey, you have a child here, remember?" Her message was rude and apologetic at the same time, but no surprise to me; I always expect rudeness from her. After all, that's why we stopped communicating; she always finds an opportunity to be rude. I told her on many occasions we do not have to like each other or be friends, but we must get along for the sake of love child.

Well, like I said, there was an apology in her message. Even though rudeness was there also, I still accepted the apology. As a matter of fact, I thought this was our moment to start off on the right foot and get along, for love child's sake. It started off really great, I must admit, but things went downhill really quick when she realized we were not able to send her money at her request. Truth of the matter and what she did not know was, we ourselves were not doing well financially. We were worst off than she could have imagined. Therefore, just as before, communication stopped again. However, this time, instead of us following her as soon as we had any extra money, we made sure we sent something for love child. It was little, but we were happy to send something. Now that we able to send funds for love child, communication started again. This time, we got to see him on the computer via the webcam. Conversations were a bit awkward for me; I felt like I was the odd one. I was the only one not related to him by blood, and that made me feel some type of way. So whenever he called us or we called him, I just said hello then moved to the side for my beloved and the kids to talk to him.

Though communication started again, it did not last very long. Just as my beloved and I expected. Love child's mom gets ill by being nice too long. If I am free to say, she acts like a spoiled kid that acts crazy when she does not get what she request. Years ago, I told her that beloved's priority is his home, and he will take care of his home first before he can do anything else. Perhaps I should not have been the one to tell her that, but if I was a gambler, I would bet that she made me mad and I threw that in her face. Yes, I know it sounds harsh, but adultery has its price.

Yet another argument between the love child's mom and I. And not that I am perfect, but I compromise for the sake of my beloved, my kids, and love child. I do not hate love child's mother, but she is not my friend or associate. I do admit, oftentimes, I have had to withhold ill words that I would love to say to her; as for her, she never resists an opportunity to be rude. Oftentimes, throwing jabs toward my beloved suggesting he is a deadbeat dad. I let her believe whatever she wants because what goes on in our home and in our life is not her business or anyone else's. My beloved always wants to do more for his love child and

I support him. However, circumstances were beyond his or my control.

We heard that love child's mother was publicly calling beloved a deadbeat; however, we were not moved. We knew the truth, and the truth made us free. My beloved and I came to the conclusion that if love child grew older and wanted to be in our lives, then and only then will we be able to show him how wrong his mother was. At that moment, after the last argument, I found peace in not communicating with love child's mother. After the last clash between her and me, my beloved said to me, "Honey, I do not know how you do it. No matter what she does, you still forgive her."

Yes, that is true. Time and time again, she has been rude to me in some way or another, always finding it necessary to remind me of her past relationship with my beloved husband. Or speaking ill toward our family. No matter what it was, whenever she came back and apologize and give her sad story about her attitude, I accepted it and forgave her.

First of all, as a Christian, my heavenly Father instructs us to always forgive. Early on, through the beginning of this horrible situation, I learned that forgiveness is for me. In order for me to move on and survive my beloved being unfaithful to me, I had to forgive and leave the vengeance to the Lord. So yes, I forgive every time even when forgiveness is not asked of me. Speaking of forgiveness, my beloved and I had a moment of truth. We have come a long way in our relationship and our marriage. So we wanted to make sure that anything we had hidden in our past do not affect us in our future. I opened up to him about my infidelity; he already knew of some of it, but there was more to tell. It was not easy pouring my heart out to him; after all, he was the reason I stepped out of my usual character. He also shared some things that was unknown to me. I thought I knew it all, but turn around, I knew nothing. Nonetheless, the moment was painful, but relieving, both of us felt weight off our shoulders. Not only did I forgive him, but I forgave others who did not even ask for my forgiveness.

After the moment of truth, healing had truly began for my family. I often heard the saying, "We all have bones in our closet" or "let dead dogs lie." However, I prove this to be a lie and a tactic of deception. We all do not have to have bones in our closet, and you do not need to let dead dogs lie. In fact, you need to clean out your closet and wake those dead dogs and give them a proper burial. Finally I felt free, free to move in the things of God. I made up in my mind that I was going to live a life holy and acceptable to God and serve Him with all my heart. I did not want to give the enemy any room or opportunity to disrupt my marriage again. Now I can say this without a shadow of doubt for myself, and I hoped it was the same for my beloved. Somewhere inside, deep, deep down was a little doubt that hubby may have some bones, but in my efforts to move forward, I accepted all he said.

With love child still on our hearts in spite of his mom, we decided to reach out to her so that we can get a goodie box to him for the second time! After my beloved and I saw our finances getting into a better place, we decided to go and buy love child some things. We were going to send it to him to have for the change of the season. Love child's mom had no idea what we were planning and decided to go off on us. Well, that pissed me off and burned all my gears!

The goodie box that we had prepared for love child, I politely unpacked that and gave the stuff to my middle son. My son ended up having a duplicate of some stuff, which was crazy, but it was not going to kill him. I refuse to send stuff to love child after his mother disrespected me. So many times I have told myself, "I am happy we don't live near her." I am convinced she would have forced me to strangle her and make an absolute fool out of myself.

One evening, I sat down and thought, *I need to forget this child exists.* When it seemed like a good idea, that was a mission impossible! I always try my best to do what is right, but it seems as if right comes at a cost and my pennies were low. My beloved and I rarely talked about love child, but I was always trying to get in his head to figure out if he was thinking about him. Knowing the father that he is, even though he doesn't express his thoughts about his love child to me, I know he thought about him. Some moments, I was okay that the well-being of his child was on his heart, and some moments it made my stomach wobble. No worries, though, I was working on myself; I kept these nasty feelings before the Lord, always asking for help. Create in me a pure heart and renew the right spirit within me was my daily bread.

After some time had passed, another message from love child's mom came through. Immediately, I thought, "Oh, I really should have blocked her on all access points!" However, deep down inside, I knew she would make contact and I was anticipating it. My anticipation was not with good intentions at all. I was waiting for her to come back and for me to show her I am what's important to my beloved. Well, if she had not taken so long, that would be where my heart was, but since she took long, it gave me time to deal with my motives. By the time she contacted me, I was not about proving a point, but about making things right so my husband can be involved in his child's life and my kids to build a relationship with their brother.

Now I still had some issues that I have never confronted, but I was willing to set them aside for my family's sake. Love child's mom contacted us because she said love child wanted to come and live with us. Now this would have been a grand opportunity for me to unleash the flesh, but instead, I decided to exercise love and control. I told her that I would get back to her, as if I needed to talk with my husband. From the moment she asked me, I knew that the ball was in my court. When I told my beloved what she wanted, he looked at me as if he was waiting for my answer. I know it would be difficult, but I said yes, love child can come live with us. When I said that, my husband took a sigh of relief and then put a big smile on his face. I knew that he would be happy!

During the course of the next few months, after school had closed for love child, it was time. We had not seen him for a couple good years. You would think love child would have forgotten about us, but when he pulled to our house, the look on his face was priceless. The little guy was so happy to see us that tears began to drop from his eyes. I reached out to hug him, and he ran into my arms. He held me like a child would hold a parent that they have not seen in a long time.

Undeniably, my heart melted; of course, I responded with the love of Christ. This was a big step for me just a few days after love child's arrival, I started to experience shortness of breath. This was all during the summer break, but I started to think about when summer break was over, the time for him to attend the same school as my middle son, the time for me to register him as my stepson. So much craziness was parading in my head. I was getting worked up over what I thought others would be thinking, giving the fact that love child and my middle son was the same age. I can tell you, there was a full-blown battle going on in my mind.

There were times when I had to tell my own self, *chill!* Love child did not give much contribution to my mind battle, but he did start to make me feel that letting him come was a mistake. Love child began to ask questions and make statements that I felt was his mother's place to settle. He did not feel as if this was all fair; in his head, he felt that his mother and father should be together. He was not able to register how his mother has a husband and his father has a wife made sense. Now, I was trying my very best not to be the one to answer him; in my head, I could not put together ways to answer him like he is a nine-year-old.

If I had answered this kid, my answers were sure to come out like a nine-millimeter bullet!

While I was taking him to get his immunization in preparation for school, Mr. Love Child had come to his breaking point and needed direct answers. He took it upon himself to ask me why his mother and father are not together. In this moment, I had to take a deep breath; immediately I thought, "Lord, why me?"

After my brief sit down with my Heavenly Father, I looked at love child and said, "I will let your father answer." I then smiled and ran back at the Master's feet; I needed a special anointing to recover from this moment! Now here we go, as love child's father, my husband came and sat with us. Love child had this innocent look on his face, as if our conversation had never happened. At that moment, I took a look deep down in his soul and I did not like what I saw; at that moment, I thought, "This kid is being used by the enemy." Anyhow I thought, *Let me get my husband up to speed because I do not want to deal with this conversation again.* Now, when I told my husband what he asked, he could not help but to smile in shock. I did smile in return, but my smile was a deal with this mess type of smile.

Just a few months after love child lived with us, I wanted to send him back home to his mother. I was open to him living with us to bond with his father and brother, but he was too dependent for a nine-year-old. I know he was not my son, but I expected him to act on the level of at least my nine-year-old who was the same age as him. He came with a whole lot of flaws, which did not bother me too much during the early months of him living with us; however, he became a burden to me. It did not feel fair to me that I needed to deal with so much frustration from him. I do understand he is a kid, but he was dishing out stuff that I do not even get from my own sons.

When I told his mother I was sending him back, she was not at all happy to hear that. In fact, she demanded to speak with his father. Well, I invited my beloved to come to the phone and speak with her, but he insisted that he do not have anything to talk to her about. She had in her mind that this was just my idea and his father will have something different to say. When he was not in agreement with me sending love child back, he understood my frustration and did not want love child to be a burden to me. My husband has never tried to force me to accept love child; in fact, he had accepted my standpoint and always took my feelings into consideration.

During the time love child was living with us, there were huge improvement in his overall character. He learned things that he did not know how to do before he came in to live with us. He always struggled in school, but I believe that over time, that, too, will improve. Therefore, although I had already made the announcement that I was sending him back home to his mom, I had changed my mind. I felt that the enemy was gaining grounds over me because I allowed this kid to frustrate me like an adult would. With this thought in mind, I changed my prayers concerning him during my prayer time. Instead of me crying to God, asking Him to help me with my feelings, I began to ask God to give him wisdom, knowledge, and understanding, then immediately, I saw change. His mom had no idea I have had a change of heart, so she messaged me saying we need to make arrangements to get him home. She wanted us to meet her halfway financially on his travels, but I disagreed. Before she sent him, I made sure stressed to her that we cannot afford to contribute to him traveling back and forth so if she wanted him, she had to make a way on her own.

While love child was living with us, we celebrated his birthday with him for the first time! For his birthday, we bought a cell phone for him. This cell phone was more of a need for him than a want. In order for his mom to communicate with him, she messaged him on my cell phone; after a while, that was annoying. So we gave him his own cell phone so she can message him whenever she want, and she was free to talk to him about whatever she wanted. While in communication with him, she told him that she was coming to get him for a visit. Love child was under the impression that he would be with his mom for the summer and would return before school. Just a few days after school had closed for the summer break, love child was gone, his mother came and took him back with her.

At that moment, the entire house was happy he left. It was as if peace had returned to the atmosphere. I thought it was a weird feeling, and I was being extra, but I was not the only one that felt the peace. My husband and sons all said, "Wow, it feels good that he is gone." I then turned to my husband and said, "Honey, sorry but *never* again." It was such a relief for me that he left that inside. I said, "I will never let my husband's outside kids live with us again." I unconsciously said "kids" as if he had more than one, then I said, "Boy, I hope my husband doesn't have any other kids out there!"

Well, with love child gone, our family returned to our regular routine. We often clowned on each other, saying they miss love child. Well, time passed, and the kids were getting ready to return to school. I could not help to give God thanks that my middle son can get more things for school since we did not have to get things for love child. From love child left, his mother never contacted us to say if they had reached their destination, nor did she discuss what her plans were as far as love child next school. She was not giving any information, and I was not asking for anything, so life continues.

Just when I thought I was entering into a comfort zone, the water raged against me once again. One day, after a very fun road trip and soccer event, my beloved sat me down to give me some news.

"Honey, I need to talk to you," he said.

My response was bubbly with no concern in my voice; we were in a good place, so I did not expect to hear nothing that would be so bad.

"This is serious," he said. Still that did not change my tune. However, I threw my legs in the chair to give him my attention. He proceeded to tell me that one of his friends from back in the Bahamas messaged him to tell him that a young lady was saying he is the father of her child. At this time, my heart fell beneath the floor. My mouth fell open and the question "Did you sleep with her?" left my voice box. His answer, "Yes, I did, I am so sorry, honey." At this moment, I felt super stupid!

It's not as if I did not have information on my husband and this young girl, but I did not have information that I could have act upon. After nine years, this mess resurfaced, why, Lord? For the next couple of days, it felt as if I was back to square one. It took me years to live and be at peace with love child no. 1; now that I am comfortable, there may be love child no. 2. I was sure this was an attack from hell. The next few days was filled with tears of grief, torment, and loads of pain. I was confused because a few weeks ago, the Lord spoke to me and told me to tell my story. There was not the question that I would do it because obviously God was up to something. When I got the instructions, I was ready to obey, but after this, I wanted to quit!

I was about to drown in depression; the enemy was having a field day in my head. My husband was doing his best to comfort me with no success. Before I got this news, I listened to Periscope just about every day then I went to not listening at all. My husband noticed the change and with an unction from Holy Spirit, he continued to try to encourage me. He reached for my phone and pulled up Periscope, as if he knew how to operate it! What he thought was a random periscope was a divine message from God. I was tired of him trying to push me to tune in to the broadcast he had pulled up so I just began to listen. The broadcast was not someone who I would listen to or even someone that I knew; I did not care I watched it anyway to satisfy my beloved. As I proceed to listen in the woman of God said, "There are some of you on here, God wanted me to tell you that the thing from the past He uncovered. He said He did it so that you can properly heal." From that moment, I shifted mode; I went from offense to defense.

Dealing with a child from infidelity is not easy, but if you want to survive it, you must be intentional about your healing. I sought the Lord with my whole heart; I gave it all I had. Yes, my flesh wanted nothing to do with these innocent kids, but my spirit was the one I had to commit to. A friend asked me, "How can you do it? I had to stop and think about it, then Holy Spirit gave me the answer! Galatians 5:22–23 says, "But the fruit of the Spirit is love, joy, peace, forbearance, kindness, goodness, faithfulness, gentleness and self-control. Against such things there is no law." If I had a problem accepting and loving these kids, then I did not have the fruit of the Spirit.

Consumed by the Claws of the Enemy

Well, as we were driving home one day, hubby and I were discussing one of his family members. This woman whom I have grown to love and to call my auntie had many kids with her husband that were not hers, and she always went over and beyond for them. Hubby was saying that is how things supposed to be, but my thing was this. It is easy for her to take care of his kids because they existed before her. However, in a case where a child came within a marriage, it is not so easy. What did I say that for, hubby began fuming out the mouth and started cursing at me; he will take care of his children and *no* one can stop him. I really did not engage in the conversation any longer as I know it was not going to end well. However, in my mind was another thing going on. I had planned that as soon as I reach home, I was going to pack my stuff and have my sister come get me.

I said nothing to him at that point; we were just a few minutes from home. Perhaps it would give him time to cool down. Well, we pulled up in the driveway; I went in the house and greeted the in-laws as if nothing happened. I marched straight in our room; hubby was behind me, and as soon as we both got through the door, I said to him, "I am leaving." All of a sudden, I was tossed on the bed and hubby jumped on top of me; he took me by the throat and began to choke me out. Very faintly I called out, "Help, help." No one came to help me. I then began to talk to God, "Lord, am I going to die like this?" Then I felt a release; he let me go and said, "You are not leaving me." After all that, the decision to stay and fight went out the window. As I laid my head to rest, I thought to myself, "My mother was a battered woman. I refuse to be a battered wife. I am going to leave this man." From that moment on, I just had to get my head prepared. The thought of being without him was scary as he was the only man I knew, so I was emotionally and physically tied.

I felt so crazy; I was so quick to say I was going to fight for my marriage, but I did not know what lied ahead. I did not sign up for this; perhaps it would have been better for me to leave from the beginning. At this point, I have to lean on the Lord. I need His strength! Just a few weeks later, I was preparing to celebrate my birthday; nothing could go wrong. I was sure that the end of the road had come so the future was bright. My birthday had come and again; hubby and I was in another argument. I was crushed on the one day I was sure was going to be a good day. We were arguing again over this new baby. I was tired, tired of arguing; that is when I decided to take a walk on the beach. I did not tell anyone where I was going. I just needed a moment. The beach was just a walk away from where we lived at the time, so I was at my destination in no time. I sat on the sand and gazed on the beautiful waters. I could not help but to admire the beauty of the sea. However, that came to an end very quickly because I burst out crying out to God, "Lord, please help me!" I was gone for about an hour, and if the sand flies did not join me, I would have been longer. Unfortunately, the sand flies needed their moment, and we could not occupy the space in harmony, so I had to leave.

As I returned home, everyone was inquiring on where I was; apparently, they were looking for me. "I was on the beach" was my answer—no other questions after that and no other explanation needed, at least to my in-laws. As I joined my husband in our bedroom, he greeted me with another argument about where I was and why I did not tell anyone where I was going. I really did not have any response for him as he was the cause of my misery. However, the silence opened a can of worms. My beloved husband began to call me every name outside my birth name; he even failed to call me a child of God. At that point, I was numb; it was the worst birthday in my entire life at that point, but after all the cussing, he said one thing that pierced my heart to the core. My beloved husband, whom I took to be my soul mate, the man whom I loved dearly, said to me, "I wish you would die!" I dropped to my knees; I could not utter a word but my heart said wow! I believed that moment was the death of me; my soul was shattered. My heart stopped aching; all the pain left my body for real; this time, I was numb.

In the midst of all my pain, I tried to do everything I can to please God, which in my eyes, doing right by the love child. Times were tough, but I tried to make sacrifices to help support this child. For a moment, I came under condemnation because my husband became absent in his life. When the Lord turned my husband around, that turn around came with wisdom. My husband decided within himself that if I am not comfortable with the child, he will keep his distance until I was ready to embrace him. Many would think this was wrong and ungodly, and I did too. However, one day the Lord spoke to me and said, "Do not worry my child, I allowed Abraham to send his love child away on the account of Sarah" (Genesis 21:12).

Comfort came to me swiftly because I know within myself that I was not doing evil with this child. I was still experiencing much hurt and pain; I needed healing. How can I give myself to this child if I am not in the right head space? I preferred to be distanced from this child rather than to mistreat him. My husband's decision to distance himself was wise; a man's priority is with his wife.

After a very difficult evening, the day prior it was time for me to rest to take on the next day. Work was always something I looked forward to going to, as during work hours, I did not have much time to think about my mess. As always, I put on my mask and killer outfit and head off to what I can call my sanctuary at the time. My workplace was a ball of confusion in itself, but yet, I was still able to find comfort there. As I was working this particular day, I called in for one of the techs from our local phone company to come in and check out our phone system as we were having issues. I was the receptionist at the time, so I walked him through the issues we were having. I was all about getting the work fix, but he had something else on his mind. I have always been able to shut flirts down; in fact, I shut this one down before, but this moment, I didn't—not that I couldn't, but I didn't.

I decided to flirt back, and as I was engaging, the only thing I was thinking about were the words my husband spoke the previous night: "I wish you would die." After months of hurting and feeling worthless, this little flirt made me feel kind of good. The tech left his personal number with me when I met him on a previous visit so after feeling rejected by my husband, I decided to use the number and reach out to the tech outside of work issues. At the moment of hurt, pain, and rejection, the thing that was responsible for my pain I found myself embracing. How was it that the thing I always hated I began to embrace? In the middle of my fight, I let my guard down and started to be consumed by the enemy. In this moment, I heard the Lord say, "No, do not do it," but did I listen? My response was "Lord, He did not reject none of these girls, he did not turn away from none of them, so I will not turn from this." And as I spoke, I felt what I was doing was right and acceptable. I felt that, hey, my husband cheated on me, so now he will feel what it is to be cheated on. Now somehow in the middle of all this, I still continue to pray to God to help me. I was binding and rebuking divorce, then at some point, what felt right did not feel right anymore. I felt conviction; it is like for a moment, my eyes were clouded, my judgment was contaminated.

Now, on top of the hurt of my husband's infidelity, I was operating against my own belief, and if it made sense, against my own will. Romans 7:23 says, "But I see another law at work in my body, warring against the law of my mind and holding me captive to the law of sin that dwells within me." I went from being cheated on to cheating! And it was not even that I was attracted to this other man, but he gave me an opportunity to take revenge. I was consumed with the idea of revenge that I began to fight against myself. It was like two people operating from one body! In one head I am thinking, "Boy, when my husband find out he is going to trip out" and in another head, "I was crying. Why did I do this, no stop." I was a fight between the evil twin and the good twin, and the evil twin was stronger because I was hurt. I felt rejected. After the actions of the evil twin, the good twin would go home and cry to sleep.

Every day I made up my mind that this was it, but my husband made it difficult. There was no end to him hurting me. A few times I told him, "I am going to leave you," and yes, I was mentally preparing an escape plan. It was not because I was running to the arms of another, but because I saw no sight of change in my husband. I know what it was to be loved; I knew what it was to be protected, so it was hard for me to conform to this misery. I just did not know how much more I could bear. Now even though I wanted to leave, I told my husband I was going to leave; now I did not know how to because I have been entangled with another man. I was worried about what people would say about me; I did not want it to be said that I left my husband for another man, so I stayed a little while longer.

As the good twin continued to cry out to God and pray, I started to distance myself from this dreadful entanglement. However, my husband had threatened to kill me, so I was done. It was time for me to leave. I called my sister; she had made arrangements for me to stay at a friend of hers house a few months prior to when she learned hubby busted my lips. Then I called my pastor to let him know what I was doing. Now my pastor said to me, "Sister Meltoria, now do not let no one influence you. Do not let anyone tell you what to do with your husband. You may want to leave now, but you will know when to go back and do not let anyone stop you."

"Okay" was my response. So my sister came and picked me up as I dropped our car off to where hubby was busy, gambling. I also had with me the gun that hubby said he will shoot me with; I took it to the local police station just to be safe.

The island was small, so I know that leaving our house did not mean I would be out of his reach. Well, somehow, he notices that the car was parked outside where he was, and it should not have, so shortly after I had settled at my sister's friend's house, my phone rang.

"Where are you?" he asked.

I replied "I left you."

Oh, it was on after that! He started cussing me out again, but this time I did not have to listen. My phone was about to explode from him texting and voice messages. One minute he was threatening me and the next minute, he was saying how much he loves me and cannot do without me. I was just crying; this was hard for me. I really did not have a game plan to be by myself and care for my children alone, and it was not about finances because I was making enough money to support myself. I was just used to doing everything with my friend, my husband.

The evening was coming to an end, but the voicemail and text messages continued. I can tell you, I did not know it was possible to text so fast. Messages were coming in one after the other; I wanted to ignore them, but I read every one. I notice, though, that the threatening messages were getting less and less, and more messages of love and compassion was coming in. I began to hear the voice of the man I fell in love with. The words "I love you so much" were words I have not heard from him in a long time. His words began to comfort my heart. As the night came in, it was time for me to rest my head. I was crying so much I could not even have conversations with the people whom I was staying with. I had with me my eldest son, Yocasta Jr., I tried to stop crying just so he did not have to see my tears, but even that could not stop the tears from flowing. Well, I finally fell asleep; the next day came in so quickly I did not feel as if I slept at all.

The next day, my in-laws called me. I knew what they were calling for. I did not want to answer, but I did not want to be disrespectful to them. They wanted to talk to me to find out where I was. I told them and they came by. They wanted me to come and talk with my husband for a minute because they said he was not taking the fact that I left too well, and they were concerned. Now I know everyone thought I should not go, but the last thing I wanted is for my husband to do anything crazy. So I went with them to talk to him. As I got back home, I saw my husband lying in the bed with his eyes blood red, a small bag packed. I sat next to him and he said, "Toya, I am leaving this island. There is no way I can live here and not be with you."

I said to him, "But look how you have been treating me, look at what you did to me. I cannot live like this."

We sat and talk about some other stuff, then he concluded, "Toya, please come back home. I promise I will change." Now I have not been gone for twenty-four hours, but I felt the sincerity in his promise so I agreed to return. Now I had packed up all my belongings so I told him, "If I come back home, you have to get my stuff and put them away!" Not only did he get all my stuff back, but he cleaned and fixed me lunch! Now I was a little afraid because I feared that this may be a trick, but I embraced it anyway.

Yes, I left my husband and returned in less than twenty-four hours. Deep down, I really did not want to divorce; as a matter of fact, I was young and did not want to go through that. However, the devil had his claws in me. I was entangled with another man. Now for me, this was all about revenge until the words "I love you" was whispered in my ears. Now for weeks I was trying to stop myself from seeing him to no avail, but these words were like poison. Once I heard them, the need for revenge was over, and I did not want to talk to this person any longer. Even though I had stopped seeing this other man, I was still feeling condemned. I went from toiling at the Master's feet for my marriage to toiling at the Master's feet for my soul. No other words could describe my feelings but filthy. My self-esteem was already shattered, but it went from shattered to nonexistent. I was messed up beyond repair; it was even difficult for me to worship. Church became a bur-

den, because every time I try to get past what I have
done, I felt condemned. I thought in my head this is
not supposed to go this way; why do I feel so horrible? I really wish I had someone I could have talked
to because I need some professional help at this point.

My husband and I felt like we were finally on a
new path; he was a new person. That brief departure
seems to have done a great deal of good. I saw noticeable
changes and the way my husband began to treat me.
He felt a need to open everything to me; he gave me all
his e-mail passcodes, his phone passcode, the code to
his social media sites. Wherever he went, he called me
and let me know where he was when he moved from
that spot he called me and let me know he moved. It
was crazy, crazy good! He said he was going to do his
best to make me comfortable and try to win my trust
back. That sounded so good, but I did not think that
was possible; I already made up in my mind that I was
never going to trust him ever again. I also told him that
I would never bear another child for him unless God
makes me. I also laid out some other request, and he
was agreeing to everything I said; finally, I felt I had
gain the upper hand.

Now I had a big issue; all the time I was mentally preparing to leave my husband, I was separating my heart from him. I didn't know how successful I was until I was feeling an emotional disconnect when I returned home. The love I was feeling was not there; I was there physically, but emotionally, I had not returned. I was already messed up in my head from all the ill words my husband had spoken to me. Every negative word he called me felt as if that was who I have become. I used the expression that he opened a can of worms, but I believe he opened a few demonic doors in my life. My husband called me an evil and wicked woman; he compared me to a female dog. These words spoken over me became who I was. I said earlier that it felt like I was fighting two personalities; however, at this point, the evil personality was still very much dominating in my life. The good personality was a small voice that prayed at night, crying out to God for help, asking God to rescue me. I felt that there was a problem, but I could not identify what it was. I was from one extramarital involvement to the next. I was crying as if someone was putting a gun to my head and forcing me to do what I did; it felt as if I had no control. I had become the ill words my husband had called me.

Ground Breaker
"Prayer"

I must give thanks to the Almighty God; He held me close even when I wanted to be let go. I cried out for help and even when it did not feel as if He heard me He did. Psalm 50:15 says, "Call upon Me in the day of trouble; I shall rescue you, and you will honor Me." He not only heard me but he helped me. Even when I walked that path of darkness, He walked me through. Yea, "though I walk through the valley of the shadow of death, I will fear no evil: for thou *art* with me; thy rod and thy staff they comfort me" (Ps. 23:4).

I was entangled in adulterous affairs crying out to God to deliver me; I did not feel as if I had the power to stop, but as I continued to cry for help, I got the strength to stop. This journey opened my eyes to a new reality. First Peter 5:8 says, "Stay alert! Watch out for your great enemy, the devil. He prowls around like a roaring lion, looking for someone to devour." The hurt I was experiencing caused me to let my guard down. No longer was I keeping watch over my soul. I was consumed by what I was going through; this left room for the enemy to devour me, but thanks be to God who cause us to triumph in His name. "The thief comes only to steal and kill and destroy; I have come that they may have life and have it to the full" (Jn. 10:10).

One thing that added to my frustration was I was not feeling any change; it did not feel as if God was hearing my cry. It did not feel as if God was going to answer my prayers. The only thing I saw was my pain, hurt, and disappointment. I did not or could not see healing, peace, or comfort. As time passed, I noticed my prayers changed from crying to God for help to spiritual warfare. Now at this time, I had no training on spiritual warfare but the Word of God declares, "Truly I tell you, whatever you bind on earth will be bound in heaven, and whatever you loose on earth will be loosed in heaven" (Matt. 18:18). So I begin to bind and loose as Holy Spirit guided.

"Through all I have been through, God have been faithful to me. For what nation is there so great, who hath God so nigh unto them, as the LORD our God is in all things that we call upon him for?" (Deut. 4:7).

The Lord has restored my marriage; it is better now than it was even before the infidelity. I thought I understood the power of prayer, but when prayer is all you have, you will understand how powerful it is. "Pray without ceasing. Give thanks in every circumstance, for this is God's will for you in Christ Jesus" (1 Thes. 5:17–18). When I needed comfort from the pain, I prayed; when I was confused, I prayed. When I was tormented in my mind, I prayed; when I was falling into sin, I prayed. Constant communication with my heavenly father rescued me.

Speaking Words of Truth

. . . .

"With the fruit of a man's mouth his stomach will be satisfied; He will be satisfied with the product of his lips. Death and life are in the power of the tongue, And those who love it will eat its fruit" (Prov. 18:20–21). My husband was not acting like a man of God, but I called him "Man of God." My husband's infidelity was no secret, and we lived in a small community where everyone knew us and what we were experiencing to some degree at that time. However, I publicly called my husband "Man of God." I even posted it on his social media pages, he had friends congratulating him and telling him he made a great choice. He had no idea what they were talking about until he went on his social media pages and saw my post. I believe that my post touched his heart; he knew the hell he was putting me through, but I choose to still speak life. Never did

I sit among my friends or family and speak against my husband. Not that I approved of his doings, neither did I accept his actions, but I knew deep down he was a good man whom I have grown to know and love.

"The wise woman builds her house, but with her own hands the foolish one tears hers down" (Prov. 14:1). I would like to believe that I was a wise woman in dealing with my family, but I cannot take any credit from Holy Spirit because He was my guide through this dark hour. As I mentioned earlier, there was a time when my husband was not gainfully employed, and I was the breadwinner at that time. My husband made some very poor choices in that moment, especially with our finances. My husband and I always had joint bank accounts; we never had my money or his money. It was always our money, but during the time of my husband's poor choices, I took it upon myself to open up a single account. I was very angry at the things he had done I had the power to dry him out financially so I was going to use it. He was furious when he found out what I had done, and I really did not care how he felt at the time. However, Holy Spirit spoke to my heart and corrected my actions. Yes, my husband was wrong in the things he was doing, but I would only add fuel to the fire that I was trying to put out.

Oftentimes, we find ourselves in positions that may try to force us to operate against God's divine order, but as wives, we must always stay in position. "For the husband is the head of the wife as Christ is the head of the church, His body, of which He is the Savior" (Eph. 5:23).

As I was going through trials and tribulations within my marriage, one thing that I practice was speaking positive. I said things like "my husband is saved, my husband is changed, my husband have wisdom." And let me say at that time he was not looking like anything I was speaking! In fact, as I spoke these things, the enemy would whisper in my ear, "That is a lie." Being a woman of God, this played on my mind a bit; I had a small conviction, but I had to believe the truth. Facts were that my husband was not saved, my husband was foolish, and there seem to be no change in sight. If we are going to believe, we must believe the truth and God's word is truth. "And the truth was that I shalt also decree a thing, and it shall be established unto thee: and the light shall shine upon thy ways" (Job 22:28). So then I knew that I was not lying but making declarations that had to go forth into the earth and manifest because the word of truth said once I declare a thing it shall be established.

As it is written: "I have made you a father of many nations." He is our father in the sight of God, in whom he believed the God who gives life to the dead and calls into being things that were not (Rom. 4:17). In this passage, God was reminding Abraham that he is the father meaning you have authority, call things that are not as though it were. The enemy tried to stop me from using my authority and power to call things into existence. I have given you authority to trample on snakes and scorpions and to overcome all the power of the enemy; nothing will harm you (Lk. 10:19). The enemy knew that as long as I spoke things that are not as though it was, my future would become my now. Yes, you want to speak positive but even in doing that, we must pay attention to our words. (My husband is going to be saved. My husband is going to come home.) If we continue to speak these words, our life will continuously be trying to catch up to what we are saying. When God spoke to create the world He said let there be, and it was (Gen. 1:3) God spoke the future into the now! I decreed and declared that my husband is saved, my husband have wisdom, no longer am I looking for the day for these things to happen. I spoke my future into my now!

Power in the Seed

After nine years from the time I found out of my husband's infidelity, the Lord spoke to me and said it is time to tell the story. I did not think that I would have to, but Abba Father required me to do so. As I was reflecting on my past events, Holy Spirit showed me myself sitting in church preparing to sow a seed. On the church envelope, I wrote, "Restore my marriage." When I saw that I said "wow" indeed, this was something that I did very often. People were sowing for house, car, and other material things, but I was believing God to restore my marriage. I had great teaching on the Kingdom principle of sowing and reaping. I had never heard testimonies of anyone who sowed on behalf of their marriage, but I was desperate and was willing to try anything. As I reflected, I remember sowing $20 seed, sometimes a $50 seed even as great as over $1,000. I did not know if it was going to work or not, I just knew there was power in the seed.

The seeds that I have sown I did not watch; I sowed and left it. I did not know when it grew. "Jesus also said, 'The kingdom of God is like a man who scatters seed on the ground. Night and day he sleeps and wakes, and the seed sprouts and grows, though he knows not how. All by itself the earth produces a crop—first the stalk, then the head, then grain that ripens within" (Mark 4:26–28). Now because of the sins of both my husband and me, I believe the Lord stripped us of all our finances and possessions. First my husband lost his job, then we lost our home and transportation. Yes, I worked for some time after my husband's infidelity, but eventually, I lost my job also. As you can imagine, this was a difficult but trying time for me and my family. However, we never went hungry; we were never without clothes on our backs and a warm place stay. David said I was young and now I am old, yet I have never seen the righteous forsaken or their children begging bread (Ps. 37:25). I did not think my seeds were bringing forth harvest, but Holy Spirit made it known to me that the seeds I have sown was not only for my marriage restoration, but to keep my family on the journey.

"For God so loved the world that He gave His only begotten son that whosoever believe in Him shall not perish but have everlasting life" (John 3:16). It was through God's seed that we have everlasting life. I always heard this scripture reference used to show how much God loved the world; however, the Holy Spirit showed me within this same passage the power of the seed. In order for us to be redeemed from the disobedience of one man, God our creator had to give up something of value. The seed had power, the power to overcome the world's greatest challenge, which was death.

"For just as through the disobedience of the one man the many were made sinners, so also through the obedience of the one man the many will be made righteous" (Rom. 5:19). As I was preparing to release my story, I heard Holy Spirit say, "Call for seed." Now I was not too happy with this because I know how people get when it is time to sow. People love harvest time to reap, but getting some people to sow is like pulling a wisdom tooth. I would have been fine with sharing my story without calling for seeds, but I came to understand that this was not about me. God sent His seed, but even the seed had to exercise obedience. In

1 Samuel 15:22, Samuel said that obedience is better than sacrifice. The seed was sent forth to redeem God's people but before it did that it had to go in the earth and die before it could have brought forth harvest. For as Jonah was three days and three nights in the belly of a huge fish, so the Son of Man will be three days and three nights in the heart of the earth (Mat. 12:40).

Seeking God's Face

"For I am afflicted and needy, And my heart is wounded within me" (Ps. 109:22). I was so worn out from fighting, my mind was messed up my heart felt broken beyond repair. My family and I had moved to a new country; this was not something we really planned, but I believed it was necessary. It has taken some time for me to adjust to the new area, even after one year, we still did not find a church to settle in. I was a woman who was always active in the church, and not being active was driving me crazy. I had so much extra time on my hands; all this was time to think about the hurt, the pain, the issues—all the negative it was hard to see the light at the end of the tunnel. I was at a point where I gave up. I gave up as in I did all I could have done, and I had no more to give. I spent many months trying to be healed, trying to act as if I was over the hurt and pain. Not for myself really, but I was trying to be over it for my husband. God hath raised him to be so loving and compassionate towards me once again, I felt sorry that I was still messed up.

On this one particular day, I went before the Lord. Psalms 55:22 says, "Cast your cares on the LORD and he will sustain you; he will never let the righteous be shaken." I was done trying to fix things, so I gave it all to God. At this moment, I did not know how to fix in position to pray, so I just went before God like I would talk to my friend. Lord, you know what I am going through; I cannot take it any longer. If you cannot fix this, then it cannot be fixed, and I will be okay with that. I am tired of the fight; I cannot do it any more I give up. From now on, I submit myself to you that you may use me as you please. When I left the presence of God, I did not bring my troubles out I left them at the altar of the Lord for Him to carry. Then I started to seek the Lord. Matthew 6:33 says, "But seek ye first the kingdom of God and His righteousness and all other things shall be added unto you." Yes, I needed stuff from God, but I came to the understanding that I needed to start seeking God's face and stop seeking His hands. When I began to do this, I noticed that I started to have peace. "Whatever you have learned and received and heard from me, and seen in me, put these things into practice. And the God of peace will be with you" (Phil. 4:9).

The enemy had my mind entangled in a web; I thought that I could not control the thoughts that came to rob me of my peace but I learned that I had power even my thoughts. As the word says in Philippians 4:8, "Finally, brothers and sisters, whatever is true, whatever is noble, whatever is right, whatever is pure, whatever is lovely, whatever is admirable, if anything is excellent or praiseworthy think about such things." I began to exercise the art of replacing all the bad thoughts with good ones. Now I said it is an art because I had to be crafty with my thoughts. When the enemy reminded me of my husband saying he hates me, I had to purposely dig up the thoughts of him saying he loved me to counteract the evil thoughts. When the enemy tries to put in my head a picture that I have never seen of my husband embracing another woman, I had to dig up the thoughts of him holding me and whispering sweet words in my ears. No longer will I be enjoying a quiet moment then out of nowhere be overwhelmed by the thoughts of my husband's infidelity. I learned to take authority over my thoughts and control my emotions.

"Thou wilt shew me the path of life: in thy presence *is* fulness of joy; at thy right hand *there are* pleasures for evermore" (Ps. 16:11). I found joy and comfort in His presence, so I dwelled there often. No longer did the enemy have room to torment my mind no longer did the enemy have power over my emotions because, in his presence, there is peace.

War Strategy

"Put on the full armor of God so that you can take your stand against the devil's schemes. For our struggle is not against flesh and blood, but against the rulers, against the authorities, against the powers of this dark world and against the spiritual forces of evil in the heavenly realms" (Eph. 6:11–12). In these two passages of scripture, the Bible is telling us that there is more going on that meets the eye. Our battle is not with the physical, so it cannot be fought physically. Spiritual, battles need to be fought spiritually, fighting in the spirit means staying on your knees in prayer. The enemy is crafty, and many times we do not see the attack coming and we are not ready for the battle. I found myself in this position; I never worried about my marriage facing trouble. I was a minister in church, but I never thought to cover my marriage or my husband in prayer. The Bible teaches us in 1 Peter 5:8 that we must be alert and of sober mind. Your enemy the devil prowls around like a roaring lion looking for someone to devour. I must be honest, I was not alert I was deep in sleep concerning my marriage. The thing we fail to pray over the enemy will prey on, no exceptions.

When I was on the front line of the battlefield over ten years ago, I called upon my help, Lord Holy Spirit who guided me to fight and lead me to victory. At that time, I had no idea what I was involved in. I did not know I was fighting a spiritual war, and neither did I know I had the power to win. However, over ten years later, I was summoned to war by the Lord of host (Ps. 46:7). Not that I needed to fight for my marriage again, but I needed to round up the warriors (wives), train them to fight then take over the enemies' camp. Initially, the task was seemingly great until Holy Spirit showed me that I have been in this battle before and won!

When the enemy attacked my marriage, he came in full force with the blink of an eye, my world got turned upside down. Felt like the gates of hell opened against me. I could not understand why the Lord allowed this to happen to me. The human spirit can endure in sickness, but a crushed spirit who can bear? (Proverbs 18:14). Being diagnosed with an STD, finding out my beloved was unfaithful, learning that there was a baby as a result, I was wounded. Soldiers do not go to war wounded; if I was going to fight for my marriage, I needed a little healing. When all this was uncovered, I was pregnant and going into delivery shortly after. I was not in the position to outburst because I had a newborn I had to tend to. As I looked back, I am happy it was so I believe I was saved from causing another battle that I did not need to fight. I had time to calm down and cry out to God; yes, I was shattered, but I was not broken.

In the middle of all the hurt, pain, and injustice I felt, I was still able to dig deep down and forgive. It was easy to forgive my husband because I was in right standing with God during this time, not saying that forgiving the other woman was easy, but I had to do it. There were times when I found myself having anxiety attacks when I get around the young lady who was pregnant for my husband. This occurred on many occasions, then I realized she was living rent-free in my head. I had to take control or else my suffering would not end. One night, as I was crying out to the Lord, I asked Him to help me to forgive everyone! Unforgiveness is like a cancer; it will eat at you bit by bit from one area to the next, but I could not allow that.

It is foolish to go into a battle not knowing your enemy or the weapons your enemy have. When going into battle, armies often check out whom they are going into battle with. They identify their defense and their weaponry so that they can identify how to not only fight but defeat. In Matthew 7:16, it says "You can identify them by their fruit, that is, by the way they act. Can you pick grapes from thorn bushes, or figs from thistles?" So then we now know that yes my husband have committed adultery therefore he is influenced by the *spirit of adultery*. If you are dealing with a spirit of adultery, then you will not go physically trying to attack your husband or attack the other woman whom he would have been involved with. You know that firstly there are things going on in the spirit realm, and you are dealing with a spirit. You can cry all the tears you have inside of you; nothing will change unless you take force. From the days of John, the Baptist until now the kingdom of heaven has suffered violence, and the violent take it by force (Matt 11:12).

I have never been to a real war, but I have watch many war videos. One thing that I see is common whichever side of the fence you are on soldiers are on the lookout. First Peter 5:8 says, "Stay alert! Watch out for your great enemy, the devil. He prowls around like a roaring lion, looking for someone to devour." As I have been dealing with many wives who are fighting infidelity, I notice that there was a common spirit at work *spirit of anger*. When I was in the fight for my marriage, many times I had to deal with my husband's anger, as if I did something wrong! My husband and I were together five years before marriage and six years before acts of unfaithfulness were exposed. Never one day in eleven years did this man curse me out or even raised a finger at me. However, after I found out about his infidelity, a beast came out and that beast did not love me. Many days I cried not always because of what was done but because of what was said. And at that time, it affected me greatly because I had no knowledge of what I was dealing with. The only thing I could have concluded from what I was dealing with was my husband hates me.

"In the beginning was the Word, and the Word was with God, and the Word was God" (John 1: 1). The word in this text is the son of God, whom He gave that we may not perish but have everlasting life (John

3:16). Jesus Christ was the solution to a problem before the problem existed. Even before you had a problem in your marriage, God already had the solution. Now one thing we must understand is not everyone will embrace the solution. However, you can make up in your mind that it is not going to be you that you will embrace the solution that God set in place for you to win.

Developing a Prayer Technique

As I stated before, in 2012, I was in a new place far away from everything that was familiar to me. Prior to that, I was in a place of comfort where I called home. I was very active in the church I attended so when I moved away from my home and church, I was not active in church any longer and that I was not accustomed to. I did not have a pastor to run and cry to when I was spiritually frustrated. I did not know a church sister whom I could call to pray with. This may seem like a negative situation, but I believe the Lord took me out of my comfort zone for a purpose. I was saved for almost ten years at this time, but when I had no pastor to run to, no sister to pray with I was compelled to have an intimate relationship with the Lord. I was going through a storm, and when I had no one to talk to, I went into my bathroom and began to cry out unto the Lord. I was always used to a formal prayer life that started off like this: Dear Heavenly Father, I come before you! At the place where I was I did not even have the strength to begin praying in that manner, it was then I learned to talk to God like a friend.

"Lord, I know that I have done some things that you were not pleased with, but I faithfully served You the best way I knew how. How did I end up in this strange place so far away from home? We really did not want to come here, but according to your Word, the steps of a righteous man you order. I am thirty-one years old and seem as if I cannot accomplish anything, and as old as I am now, I don't have time to do anything. Lord, I never thought it would be so hard to find a new church; how am I going to survive spiritually if I don't find a new church to call home? I asked God these questions in no formal manner, but I really wanted an answer."

I didn't really expect the Lord to answer right away, but I concluded like this: "Lord, I need your help, I need you to change my situation only you can do it, and if you can't do it, it cannot be done. Lord, tonight I give myself over to you use me as you please speak to my heart your servant is listening."

Yes, I wept, but I was confident that the Lord was listening to me. I spoke as if he was near; I gave up my usual way of praying for an unusual way of prayer. Just one week after I wept before the Lord, I connected with a young lady who said she had a word from the Lord for me. At that point, I was all ears because I really needed a word from the Lord; I was hungry for His word. When the young lady began to speak to me, I was astonished because she was answering every question I asked the Lord in my intimate session with him. I was almost in tears because I was so happy to hear from Him, but I was too busy jumping inside because God was answering me back. Yes, I was saved for over ten years, but I have never had such an experience where God answered me in such a short period. I have heard from others that God has spoken, but I was excited to have a personal experience. Let me not forget to add not only did God answer my prayer, He also told me something I did not know. After delivering the message of the Lord, the young lady said to me, "Meltoria, you are a prophet." Now I heard her, but those words did not excite me too much as I always believed that a prophecy should be a word of confirmation. Yet, on the other hand, I did not reject the word as she was so on target with answering all the questions I had put to God in my intimate moment with him. I always thought in the back of my mind, could she be right?

During my valley experience, I know that it was crucial for me to pay attention to my spiritual life because I was not actively attending church as I previously did. I began to study God's word like never before. Yes, I know the scripture that says study to show thyself approved, but I was so busy with everyday life I did not spend too much time studying. Well, let me be honest; I did not study at all! Yes, I did do some praying, but I can honestly say now that was because that is what was done during prayer meeting, prayer! I believe that I was so spiritually frustrated because I thought my spiritual survival was based on going to church faithfully and not praying and studying privately.

I am convinced that many people who are in church today rely on corporate word, worship, and prayer to maintain their walk with the Lord, which brings me to question: are we seeking to please God or man? As I began to aggressively pay attention to my spiritual life, the Lord began to show up in ways that I have never experienced before; He sent me books that would begin to teach me things I have never heard before. Holy Spirit inspired me to watch videos and connect with people that I would have never connected with if I was still in my comfort zone. I began to develop strong study habits, and I understood God's word clearer. Yes, I continued to pray, but I always felt that there was more.

All of a sudden, I lost confidence in my prayer life and started to shy away from it completely. I continued in my studies in God's word and always listened to God's people preach or teach via social media and YouTube. I almost forgot that it was not only necessary to pray, but it was crucial for me because I needed to grow in the power of God and without prayer that was not possible. Growing up, I often heard and used the phrase, "More prayer more power, less prayer less power." At one point, this was just a phrase I heard, but God showed me the reality of it.

One night I had a dream, there was a child playing outside my house, and the child began to have an epileptic fit. People gathered around the child trying to figure out what was happening. I was inside looking out the window when someone shouted, "Call Toya, she can help." I was looking at them, but I did not go to help because I knew I had not been in prayer so I would not be able to help. A few nights later, I had another dream where a person was outside my house being tormented by a demon and my husband shouted, "Call Toya, she knows what to do." At this point, I knew the Lord was speaking to me and showing me what would happen if I am not prepared in prayer.

The dreams really awaken me to the importance of me developing a prayer life, and even though I understood that the enemy was fighting me, trying to keep me away from it. I knew that I had to push to prevail, and with confidence, I would make progress. From that point, I began to look up scriptures on prayer just to try rebuild my prayer foundation that was severed. Matthew 6:9–16 says this, "This, then, is how you should pray: Our Father in heaven, hallowed be your name your kingdom come, your will be done, on earth as it is in heaven. Give us today our daily bread. And forgive us our debts as we also have forgiven our debtors. And lead us not into temptation, but deliver us from the evil one. For if you forgive other people when they sin against you, your heavenly Father will also forgive you. But if you do not forgive others their sins, your Father will not forgive your sins." This is a prayer that I always prayed growing up as a child, and this is the prayer I taught my kids. Now this is the prayer that I would use to get my prayer life restarted.

Every night when I went to bed, I tried my best to pray even if it is just the "Our Father" prayer. And even though sometimes I would forget to pray I would wake up through the night just to get it in. As time passed, I started to mature in prayer again, not being religious but praying as I am speaking to my friend. Sometimes because of the sovereignty of God, we feel as if he is too mighty to be considered a friend, but in the book of Genesis, we see that God spoke to Moses as a friend.

In an aggressive effort to develop my prayer life, not only did I make an effort to pray without ceasing, I started to listen to a lot of prayers of others. During the night time before I go to sleep, I would tune into and listen to prayers by Dr. Cindy Trimm. Dr. Trimm's prayers were very powerful warfare prayers, and they touched many areas; her prayers were effective. Not only was I listening to her prayers, but I was also learning. I was great at studying the word so now it is time for me to inject those words into my prayers. With the help of the Holy Spirit, I began to learn the rules of engagement, not just praying but warfare prayer.

After much fasting, prayer, and studying, the Lord began to teach me in the area of healing and deliverance. I was amazed because I have never really heard of this teaching because no one really focused on this ministry. However, as I looked back at my prayer struggle, I understand why there was such a fight for me to get back into prayer. In developing my prayer life, I began to read my scriptures, study more literature, and listen to more teachings. If I wanted to develop a strong life of prayer, I knew I had to be intentional and aggressive.

I would say that I was getting better with prayer, but I know I still had work to do. I was referred to a book called *Prayer that Rout Demons* by John Eckhardt. I spent a few days reading the book hoping this would give me the help that I needed. This book was ten times better than I expected or anticipated; these prayers routed demons indeed. The words were not only strategic, but it was biblical. I was almost discouraged for a minute because these prayers were at a level I had not been before. I always struggled to arise early to pray, but that was only because I felt that I was not good at praying and I would not know what to say when I prayed. One day, I thought I could use the prayers in this book to pray! It took me a few days before I actually begin to pray each morning, but eventually, I did.

Each night before I went to bed, I used the book to pray; after I got a hang of it, I thought this would be a great time to start my early morning prayer. So then I set my alarm clock at 4:50 AM so I could be sure to wake. I pushed myself each morning to pray the prayers from *Prayers that Rout Demons*. It was a life changer for me. I started to use it so much that many of the prayers began to commit to memory. This built my confidence so high that one morning even before I opened the book, I began to pray on my own. I gave in and allow the Holy Spirit to guide me as I prayed. I prayed for people I did not know personally and things I did not think about before I entered my prayer room.

The word of God teaches that the Holy Spirit gives intercession when we do not know what to pray. This was no surprise to me because one evening as I laid in silence, I asked the Lord, "What should I pray about as I enter my prayer closet?" To no surprise, the Lord spoke to my spirit and instructed me to call His people to mail me their prayer request. At that moment, I was so excited because I felt accomplished. I have gotten my prayer life back. I can honestly say if the Lord had given me such instructions one year ago, I would have been scared out of my wits.

The Bible declares that we must enter into His gates with thanksgiving and into His courts with praise. It is the plan of the enemy to make you and me believe that you need a PhD to pray, or you need to know so many steps to prayer to get your prayers answered. This idea I believe is set in place to bring fear and intimidation to keep us away from this powerful tool—prayer. Well, the truth is that the effectual and fervent prayer of the righteous avails much. When I broke through the stronghold of intimidation and fear, I began to pray with effect and with consistency. We must constantly pray because we do not know which prayer will be the one that get answered.

Many times I feel as if I am bothering God by praying the same prayer. However, I understand that the prince of the air is always on duty, full force and in effect waiting to block prayers from getting into heaven. We must be aggressive with our prayers and be like Jacob and wrestle with the angels if we have to. Prayer is a vital part of a Christian's life; it is our way of communicating with our creator. The Lord has given us power and dominion over the earth. Yes, God is all powerful but God have given us authority over the earth so we must command or ask God to move on the earth. The enemy will fight against a healthy prayer life, but we have power and authority over him. Satan is already defeated; we must not be intimidated nor afraid of him. However, we must be intentional about prayer. Prayer in the morning, prayer in the afternoon, and prayer in the evening if we have to. Whatever we do in our Christian walk, we must ensure that prayer is included in it.

Will This Dead Marriage Live?

In Ezekiel 37, the Spirit of the Lord asked the prophet Ezekiel, "Son of Man, can these dry bones live?" Now I know many people are looking at their marriage as dead. They are ready to put it in a coffin and commit it to the ground and declare ashes to ashes dust to dust. But if we look closely at Ezekiel, we can understand that even the thing that is not only dead but dried up can live if we prophesy. Now we when the Spirit of the Lord asked Ezekiel if the dry bones can live, Ezekiel said, "O Lord God, you know." Again the Spirit of the Lord instructed him to prophesy to the dry bone. Ezekiel 37:4–6 says, "Again He said to me, Prophesy to these bones, and say to them, 'O dry bones, hear the word of the Lord!' ⁵Thus says the Lord God to these bones: 'Surely I will cause breath to enter into you, and you shall live. I will put sinews on you and bring flesh upon you, cover you with skin and put breath in you; and you shall live. Then you shall know that I am the Lord.'"

As I was going through the valley, the place where I saw my marriage dead. The Spirit of the Lord came upon me, and I prophesied to my dead marriage. At the time, I did not know what I was doing, but Lord Holy Spirit reminded me of many occasions when I said, "I will not divorce" or "My husband is a man of God." This may seem simple and of no effect, but I spoke my dead marriage to life. My husband disrespected me, not only in actions but also in his words, I was mentally and physically abused. One day I prophesied into my husband's ears and into the atmosphere. I said, "My mother was a battered woman, I WILL NOT BE A BATTERED WIFE!" From that moment on, things shifted.

When you begin to prophesy, there is a process to the dead coming to life. I believe as you begin to speak to your situation, the enemy begins to make a sound that aims to bring confusion to you. Prophesying causes things to shift and atmospheres to shake. So I prophesied as I was commanded; and as I prophesied, there was a noise, and suddenly a rattling; and the bones came together, bone to bone. Indeed, as I looked, the sinews, and the flesh came upon them, and the skin covered them over; but there was no breath in them (Ez. 37:7–8). I find that the majority of people when going through trials then tend to always speak of what is before them. For example, wives who are experiencing infidelity, always talking about what their husbands are currently doing, and talking about how they currently feeling. As I was going through that is something that I did not talk about. I did not discuss with friends and family how awful my husband was treating me or how broken and hurt I felt. Instead, I prophesied! I would like every one of you to speak in tongues, but I would rather have you prophesy. The one who prophesies is greater than the one who speaks in tongues, unless someone interprets, so that the church may be edified. There is more power in prophecy than complaining (1 Cor. 14:5).

Pain, Birth, My Purpose

After I received salvation over ten years ago, I looked forward to the day that my husband would serve the Lord as well. It was not so bad initially when I got saved, I really did not expect my husband to make the change because I did. However, I began to serve the Lord as a youth pastor and a dance minister, I began to feel a void. So many were touched and moved by what the Lord was using me to do, and yes, I was honored to be available to be used, but my husband and I were living in two different worlds. Many times, I begged my husband to come to church, come to an event I was hosting, come and hear me minister the word, come and watch me dance before the Lord, but he was not there.

As I reflect on the times, I had the opportunity to evaluate my walk with God then and now. Yes, I was a youth pastor and dance minister, but I was so busy with works that I had no relationship with my Heavenly Father. Although the ministries I oversaw seem to bear fruit, I believe I was operating prematurely. I did not have enough time to be personally grounded and intimate before I took on responsibilities in the church. I believe this is a problem that many Christians face today. As a young Christian, you have that fire that zeal to be used that you are willing to do whatever you can in the church. I believe this is dangerous because oftentimes, this can cause you to operate out of the will of God.

That point in my life came when my foundation was tested; the storm came and nearly brought my temple to destruction. I was in a bad state of mind; everything was out of sync—mind, body, and spirit was not in alignment. Proverbs 18:14 says, "The human spirit can endure in sickness, but a crushed spirit who can bear?" My Spirit was crushed, I came to the conclusion that I needed to go before my creator and tap into something I have only heard about. With transparency I went before God and I laid it all before Him. Yes He knows all about my troubles, but Psalm 55:22 said,

"Give your burdens to the LORD, and he will take care of you. He will not permit the godly to slip and fall."

I surrendered to God once again as if it was my first time to salvation. One thing I said among other things God, use me as you please. Following that moment I began to seek God like never before, in my darkest hours, I learned how to commune with Him and He communes with me. I believe in these moments my eyes were opened to see and my ears were opened to hear. I was surprised because after over ten years being saved, I did not know that I was spiritually blind or deaf. Jesus asked His disciples in Mark 8:18, "You have eyes, can't you see? You have ears, can't you hear?" Don't you remember anything at all? I most certainly believe Jesus was speaking to me!

After some years of preparation by Lord Holy Spirit, I was sitting back just thinking about I believe what I was going to cook. Then I heard a voice, "It is time to tell the story." I paused for a minute and asked, "What?" The reply was "It's time to tell the story." Now I have been living in the land of restoration for a few years, the pain and thought of my past I buried! For God to ask me to do such a thing, I know He had a plan. As I released my story on what I went through,

I felt something that I have never felt before true freedom! By the blood of the Lamb and the words of my testimony I was free (Revelation 12:11)

Living a Victorious Marriage

Many people asked, "How long before your victory?" I have been very transparent about my story, so I really wanted to give an answer, but truth is, I do not have a timeline. I remember when the gates of hell opened against me. I remember many days I cried and ask the Lord to help me, I remember wondering when will this nightmare end. I have given birth to three amazing boys; I believe if I remembered the pain of childbirth, I would only have one!

Victory is a process, and I believe everyone's process is different. I know of a lady in my small community who was having marital problems before I was. In fact, I recall looking at her and thinking, "Now that I could not do." Her husband had already moved in with another woman, and they had a child together. Meanwhile, she continued to believe this man was going to come home, she continued to exercise her faith. One day after more than five years, her husband came home. I was so happy for her something leaped in my spirit as she told me the good news. As time passed, I had the opportunity to sit with her as she told me how this crazy man returned home. Crazy as in a sweet crazy: he wanted to go everywhere she went, he wanted her to go everywhere he went, and so on. All I could do was smile with great joy. I was familiar with everything she was talking about as I have experienced the same thing.

I cried many nights unto God with no feeling or sign that He was hearing my cry or my prayers. I sewed many sacrificial seeds not knowing even if it made sense. However, one day some time ago, it was all over. My husband was a changed man; he was renewed and restored better than before. Which day that was is unknown to me, I just know the day exists!

As I have launched out and began to speak as the Lord leads, one thing I have realized. Infidelity attacked many of our homes, many of our husband's battle with addictions. Some of us are up against generational curses some against witchcraft. The spirit of adultery, lust, and perversion has consumed our husbands like a burning fire. As wives who love our husbands and have not given up on our marriages, we all have the same destination but our journeys there may be different.

I asked myself what I think to be a very valuable question: "I am happy that I stayed and fought for my marriage?" My answer is absolutely YES! Out of my journey, I was given a totally restored husband, friend, marriage, and family.

About the Author

Meltoria A. Woodside is happily married to Yocasta Woodside Sr. Together, they bore three sons, Yocasta Jr., Carlisle, and Mateo. She was born and raised in the Bahamas, then later on with her family, relocated to California.

"Above it all, she is a servant of God. She has been set over nations and over kingdoms, to root out, to pull down, to destroy, to throw down, to build and to plant" (Jer. 1:10).

Since her commission about nine years after the victory over the fight against infidelity, she heard in a still small voice, "It's time to tell the story." *What story?* she thought, then the Lord said to her, "*When Wives Fight, Families Win!*"

What she experienced with adultery she never spoke about. She was so caught up being happy she survived the pain, that she did not realize she was not totally free. However, after the call to speak she understood that by the words of her testimony she would be free (Rev. 12:11). As she begins to testify, she realizes that not only did she win, but through her testimony, others would win as well.